Top 100 Most Commonly Idioms and Phrases

for

Advanced Non-Native English Speakers

A simple and easy way to understand business idioms.

Includes:

Quick Reference List and Definitions

Example Sentences

Worksheets

Worksheet Answers

10 Parts (100 Idioms)

+10 Bonus

Top 100 Most Commonly Used Business Idioms and Phrasal Verbs for Advanced Non-Native English Speakers

Book and Cover Design by Ioana Schiopu

Printed by CreateSpace, An Amazon.com Company

ISBN-13: 978-1543229080
ISBN-10: 1543229085

Manufactured in Canada

Quick Reference
List and Definitions

Top 100 Business Idioms and Phrasal Verbs

Part 1

1. **Take the bull by the horns** = Directly attack or confront a problem or challenge.
2. **Be on the same page** = Have the same understanding or opinion about an idea or situation.
3. **Think outside the box** = Be creative, have innovative ideas; approach a situation in a new or different way.
4. **Shoot me straight** = Be very direct and honest.
5. **See eye-to-eye** = Agree about or have the same understanding on something.
6. **Bend over backwards** = Try very hard to please someone or to accomplish something.
7. **Lay it on the line** = Be very direct and precise.
8. **Back out of something** = Cancel an agreement or arrangement.
9. **Give and take** = Cooperate or compromise.
10. **Meet someone halfway** = Compromise.

Part 2

11. **Cut a deal** = Reach an agreement, make a deal
12. **Water under the** bridge = A past issue, someone's mistake, that is forgiven and is no longer a concern.
13. **At stake** = Something that can be gained or lost.
14. **Back down from something** = Retreat or give up one's position during negotiations, not continue with a threat to do something.
15. **Ball is in someone's court** = It is the decision of another person/ group in a negotiation.

16. **Beat around the bush** = Speak about something in an indirect way.
17. **Blow a deal** = Fail to make a business deal.
18. **Bog down** = Slow down and make no progress, being overwhelmed.
19. **Bone of contention** = The reason for a fight, disagreement, or dispute.
20. **Breakthrough** = Successful after overcoming a difficulty; having a revelation or an idea.

Part 3

21. **Backfire** = Have an action that you did come back at you or affect you in a negative way.
22. **Bring someone to terms** = Make someone agree to something
23. **Bring something to the table** = Have something to offer or bargain with during a negotiation.
24. **Call someone's bluff** = Make someone prove that they can actually do what they say they can.
25. **Call the shots** = Be in charge or give orders.
26. **Cave in to someone or something** = Weaken your stance and be forced to give up.
27. **Close a deal** = Reach the end of negotiations successfully.
28. **Come in high/low** = Offer too much, or offer a low amount of money.
29. **To tiptoe around someone/something** = Behave carefully toward someone because you are afraid of offending them or making them angry; avoid addressing a problem directly.
30. **Common ground** = Shared beliefs or interests.

Part 4

31. **Down to the wire** = Near a deadline, have little time remaining, approaching the end of a project.
32. **Cover a lot of ground** = Talk about all the important facts and details of something.
33. **Cut someone off** = Stop someone from saying something, interrupt.
34. **Drag on** = Be prolonged, continue for a long time, advances slowly.
35. **Drag one's heels** = Act slowly or reluctantly.

4

36. **Draw the line** = Set a limit about what will be done or discussed.
37. **Drive a hard bargain** = Unrelenting negotiation to make an agreement to one's advantage.
38. **Drive at something** = Mean something, want to say, or indirectly imply something.
39. **Fall through** = Fail, be ruined, not happening.
40. **Force someone's hand** = Make someone do something that they do not want to do.

Part 5

41. **Gentleman's agreement** = An oral, not written agreement 5 between two people who trust each other.
42. **Get behind a person or idea** = Support a person or idea.
43. **Get down to business** = Start working or doing the business at hand.
44. **Get the ball rolling** = Start an activity or action.
45. **Get the raw end of the deal** = Make an unsatisfactory deal.
46. **Get through to someone** = Make someone understand.
47. **Get to the bottom of something** = Discover or understand the real cause of something.
48. **Get to the heart of something** = Find the most important facts or core meaning of something.
49. **Give away the farm** = Offer too much during a negotiation.
50. **Give ground** = Move back or retreat from one's position.

Part 6

51. **Go against the grain** = Do things in an unconventional manner, in a way that is not generally approve.
52. **Go back to square one** = Go back to the beginning.
53. **Go back to the drawing board** = Go back and start something from the beginning; go back to the planning stage.
54. **Go for broke** = Risk everything on one big deal; try as hard as possible.
55. **Go over like a lead balloon** = Fail to obtain a positive response.
56. **Go over well** = Be liked or successful.
57. **Hammer out an agreement or a deal** = Negotiate a deal or agreement by discussing and debating the details.
58. **Hard-nosed** = Be very strict, stubborn, uncompromising.
59. **Have a card up one's sleeve** = Have crucial or sensitive

information that only revealed to benefit the person having it.

60. **Hold all the aces/cards/trumps** = Have all of the advantages.

Part 7

61. **Hold out for something/someone** = Keep resisting or refuse to give up until you get the desired results.
62. **Hold out on someone** = Refuse to give information to someone who has a right to it.
63. **In the bag** = Certain; something has been acquired.
64. **Iron something out** = Ease a problem, smooth out the details of a problem.
65. **Knock down** = Decrease a price.
66. **Lay one's cards out on the table** = Be open and honest about one's intentions.
67. **Make headway** = Make progress.
68. **Nail down the terms of an agreement** = Discuss and agree on the terms of a contract.
69. **Off the record** = Not published or revealed, a secret.
70. **Paint oneself into a corner** = A difficult or impossible situation.

Part 8

71. **Play hardball** = Act in a strong and aggressive way; behave in an unpleasant, threatening way to get what you want.
72. **Play into someone's hands** = Do something that another person can use against you.
73. **Pull something off** = Succeed in achieving something difficult
74. **Pull something out of a hat** = Get something as if by magic.
75. **Put one's shoulder to the wheel** = Start hard work.
76. **Raise the ante** = Increase what is at stake or under discussion in a dispute or conflict.
77. **A raw deal** = Treatment that is not fair.
78. **Reach a stalemate** = Arrive at a position where progress can no longer be made.
79. **Reach an impasse** = Get to a point where progress is impossible.
80. **Read between the lines** = Understand the meaning of something by guessing what is not said.

81. **A rock-bottom offer** = The lowest price that one can offer to buy something.
82. **A setback** = A change from better to worse, a delay, a reversal.
83. **Smooth something over** = Make something seem better or less severe.
84. **Speak of the devil** = When the person you were talking about suddenly appears.
85. **Stack the deck against someone** = Trick someone, to arrange things unfairly.
86. **Stand one's ground** = Maintain and defend one's position.
87. **Stick to one's guns** = Defend an action or opinion despite an unfavorable reaction.
88. **A stumbling block** = Something that prevents or obstructs progress.
89. **Sweeten the deal** = Offer something during a negotiation that is attractive to the other side.
90. **Talk someone into/out of something** = Get someone to agree to something, persuade someone to do something.

Part 10

91. **Take a stab at something** = Attempt or try something.
92. **Talk over something** = Discuss something.
93. **Throw someone a curve** = Something unexpected and unpleasant.
94. **To a T** = Exactly, nothing done wrong or left undone, perfectly.
95. **Wax and wane** = Increase and decrease.
96. **Wheel and deal** = Negotiate to buy and sell something in an almost dishonest or illegal way.
97. **Back to/against the wall** = In serious difficulty, have to give in or agree.
98. **Beggars can't be choosy** = Not reject an offer if it is the only possibility you have, especially if it is free of charge.
99. **Bide your time** = Wait for a good opportunity to do something.
100. **Odds and ends** = Bits and pieces, often small details of little value.

Part 1

Part 1 - Examples

1. v. to take the bull by the horns

Example 1: Brad wasn't happy with the manager's decision, so he took the bull by the horns and demanded to see him in order to discuss the matter.

Example 2: The magazine's sales were falling, so the owner took the bull by the horns and replaced the editor, had the layout redesigned, and brought in new writers.

2. v. to be on the same page

Example 1: Before we make any decisions today, I'd like to make sure that everyone is on the same page, we all agree that we need to make some changes to the existing contract, right?

Example 2: The CEO and the manager are on the same page, they both think that the best way to motivate employees is by positive reinforcement.

3. v. to think outside the box

Example 1: For our year-end party this year, let's not just go for dinner. Let's think outside the box. How about we take the staff skydiving?

Example 2: In order to beat our competitor in the teens' market, we need to think outside the box for promoting our product. Instead of just TV commercials, how about we arrange special concerts at high schools in the area?

4. v. to shoot someone straight / n. a straight shooter

Example 1: Shoot me straight, do we have any chance of winning the project from your company or not?

Example 2: Shoot me straight doctor, what were the results of my blood test and how bad is it?

Example 3: Mr. Smith is a straight shooter; if you want to know what really happened, you should ask him.

5. v. to see eye-to-eye

Example 1: My manager and I see eye-to-eye on most issues; we both think that company dinners are a good way for coworkers to bond.

Example 2: Mr. Jones and Mr. Smith don't see eye-to-eye on when to launch the new product. Mr. Jones thinks it should be next month, and Mr. Smith thinks it should be in 3 months.

6. v. to bend over backwards

Example 1: I have been bending over backwards for my boss so that I get a promotion next year.

Example 2: I had to bend over backwards to get the price of the product lowered for the customer so that I could make this sale.

7. v. to lay it on the line

Example 1: Ok, I am going to lay it on the line, because of your tardiness, as of May 1st, you will no longer be working with us.

Example 2: You're just going to have to lay it on the line and tell her that if the quality of her work does not improve, she will be fired.

8. v. to back out of something

Example 1: We almost got them to sign the contract, but at the last minute, they backed out.

Example 2: I have a dinner meeting with a client tonight but I may have to back out of it since I am not feeling well.

9. v. to give and take / n. give and take

Example 1: The secret to a good relationship, whether personal or professional, is to give and take.

Example 2: We had to give and take a little, but in the end we agreed on the terms of the contract.

10. v. to meet someone halfway

Example 1: I know you would like a 20% discount; I can meet you half way and give you a 10% discount.

Example 2: The supplier said they can't deliver until the end of the month, but after I explained the urgency, they met us halfway and said they could deliver mid-month.

Part 1

Instructions: Put the following idioms and phrasal verbs in the correct blanks, and in the correct form. Some may have more than one possible answer.

1. v. to take the bull by the horns
2. v. to be on the same page
3. v. to think outside the box
4. v. to shoot someone straight / n. a straight shooter
5. v. to see eye-to-eye
6. v. to bend over backwards
7. v. to lay it on the line
8. v. to back out of something
9. v. to give and take / n. give and take
10. v. to meet someone halfway

A. The deal was almost cemented, but at the last minute, the other company _____. (1)

B. This new ad has to be completely different than our competitors'. If we don't start _____, then we will lose our market share. (2)

C. In order to get my boss to come down on price, you will have _____ and increase your order. (1)

D. The two directors haven't _____ on many issues since they had a falling out a few years ago. (2)

E. A little _____ is needed in a win-win situation. (1)

F. The manager wasn't afraid _____ for his employees. He told them, if they don't improve their productivity, they would be replaced. (1)

G. I'm glad we _____ about this issue; I can now move forward and propose it to the customer. (2)

H. Even though I had _____ for the customer by

begging the supplier for a lower price, in the end, they still were not satisfied and wanted even lower. (1)

I. During the negotiation, Mr. Smith _____, and he told me that unless we would provide free delivery, the deal would absolutely not go through. (2)

J. After being consistently mistreated by my manager for no apparent reason, I decided _____ and confront him about it. (1)

Part 1 Answers

Instructions: Put the following idioms and phrasal verbs in the correct blanks, and in **the correct form**. Some may have more than one possible answer.

1. v. to take the bull by the horns
2. v. to be on the same page
3. v. to think outside the box
4. v. to shoot someone straight / n. a straight shooter
5. v. to see eye-to-eye
6. v. to bend over backwards
7. v. to lay it on the line
8. v. to back out of something
9. v. to give and take / n. give and take
10. v. to meet someone halfway

A. The deal was almost cemented, but at the last minute, the other company **backed out of it**.

B. This new ad has to be completely different than our competitors'. If we don't start **taking the bull by the horns / thinking outside of the box**, then we will lose our market share.

C. In order to get my boss to come down on price, you will have **to meet me halfway** and increase your order.

D. The two directors haven't **seen eye-to-eye / been on the same page** on many issues since they had a falling out a few years ago.

E. A little **give and take** is needed in a win-win situation.

F. The manager wasn't afraid **to lay it on the line** for his employees. He told them, if they don't improve their productivity, they would be replaced.

G. I'm glad we **see eye-to-eye / are on the same page** about this issue; I can now move forward and propose it to the customer.

H. Even though I had **to bend over backwards** for the customer by begging the supplier for a lower price, in the end, they still were not satisfied and wanted even lower.

I. During the negotiation, Mr. Smith **laid it on the line / shot me straight**, and he told me that unless we would provide free delivery, the deal would absolutely not go through.

J. After being consistently mistreated by my manager for no apparent reason, I decided **to take the bull by the horns** and confront him about it.

Part 2

Part 2 - Examples

1. v. to cut a deal

Example 1: After 3 hours of negotiating, we were able to cut a deal in regards to pricing.

Example 2: Since the two parties were unable to cut a deal, they decided to sever ties and go their own separate ways.

2. v. to be water under the bridge

Example 1: John: I want to apologize for my behavior yesterday. I'm sorry.
David: Don't worry, it's all water under the bridge.

Example 2: Chris: Sorry about this morning, I didn't mean to get so angry.
Mike: Water under the bridge.

3. v. to be at stake

Example 1: The future of our company is at stake here, if we get this contract we will double our profit.

Example 2: John: Let's play poker.
Mike: Ok! What are the stakes?

4. v. to blow a/the deal

Example 1: Eric blew the deal by coming on too strong his aggressive behavior was a turnoff for the main decision maker.

Example 2: I want to make sure we are properly prepared; we can't afford to blow this deal.

5. v. to back down from something

Example 1: They drove a hard bargain at first, but then eventually backed down and agreed to a more reasonable price.

Example 2: They threatened to sue the company, but in the end they backed down after seeing the high cost of litigation.

BONUS: **To drive a hard bargain** = to be stubborn about what you want.

6. "the ball is in (someone's) court"

Example 1: I sent the customer the lowest final prices that I could get; the ball is in his court now.

Example 2: We called the company and made an offer, the ball is in their court.

7. v. to beat around the bush

Example 1: So, I'm not going to beat around the bush, I'm sorry to inform you that your contract has been terminated.

Example 2: When delivering bad news, it is best to get straight to the point and not beat around the bush.

8. v. to bog down

Example 1: Due to the economic crisis, business has bogged down.

Example 2: The project was bogged down due to the delay in parts delivery.

9. n. bone of contention

Example 1: Whatever you do, don't bring up the fact that the part was delivered late; it is a bone of contention for him.

Example 2: The company's inability to provide local and efficient customer service repair, is a bone of contention for many of its customers.

10. n. a breakthrough

Example 1: After years of studies, the researchers finally had a breakthrough when the rats' cancer started shrinking.

Example 2: There was a breakthrough in negotiations and a deal was reached after a 3-month long dispute.

Part 2

Instructions: Put the following idioms and phrasal verbs in the correct blanks, and in **the correct form.** Some may have more than one possible answer.

1. v. to cut a deal
2. v. to be water under the bridge
3. v. to be at stake
4. v. to blow a/the deal
5. v. to back down from something
6. v. "the ball is in (someone's) court"
7. v. to beat around the bush
8. v. to bog down
9. n. bone of contention
10. n. a breakthrough

A. Ok, I'm not going _____, as of next month we will have massive layoffs.

B. After hours of negotiating, the two companies were able _____.

C. Try to smooth over the fact that we don't have local customer support; that's often a _____ for them.

D. Mr. Johnson _____ by coming on too strong, his stubbornness ultimately turned the other party against any possible positive outcome.

E. The fight that Mr. Smith and Mr. Thompson had last year is all _____; they now get along just fine.

F. Due to the industry taking a downturn this year, our business, as a result, has also _____.

G. After months of trial and error, we finally had a _____, and the machine now works flawlessly.

H. We proposed to them the absolute lowest price that we could on this deal and now _____; they'll probably get back to us within a week.

I. They threatened that they would go to our competitor, but
realistically we are the only company that produces this type of
technology, so of course they _____.

J. There's a lot _____ here if we get this contract.
It could be the difference between becoming the market leader or
having to close down the entire division.

Part 2 Answers

Instructions: Put the following idioms and phrasal verbs in the correct blanks, and in **the correct form.** Some may have more than one possible answer.

1. v. to cut a deal
2. v. to be water under the bridge
3. v. to be at stake
4. v. to blow a/the deal
5. v. to back down from something
6. v. "the ball is in (someone's) court"
7. v. to beat around the bush
8. v. to bog down
9. n. bone of contention
10. n. a breakthrough

A. Ok, I'm not going **to beat around the bush**, as of next month we will have massive layoffs.

B. After hours of negotiating, the two companies were able **to cut a deal**.

C. Try to smooth over the fact that we don't have local customer support; that's often a **bone of contention** for them.

D. Mr. Johnson **blew the deal** by coming on too strong, his stubbornness ultimately turned the other party against any possible positive outcome.

E. The fight that Mr. Smith and Mr. Thompson had last year is **water under the bridge**; they now get along just fine.

F. Due to the industry taking a downturn this year, our business, as a result, has also **bogged down**.

BONUS: **downturn** = decrease, turned for the worse, **bogged** = stopped, reached an obstacle.

G. After months of trial and error, we finally had a **breakthrough**, and the machine now works flawlessly.

H. We proposed to them the absolute lowest price that we could on this deal, and now **the ball is in their court**; they'll probably get back to us within a week.

I. They threatened that they would go to our competitor, but realistically we are the only company that this type of technology, so of course they **will back down from it**.

J. There's a lot **at stake** here, if we get this contract. It could be the difference between becoming the market leader or having to close down the entire division.

Part 3

Part 3 - Examples

1. v. to backfire

Example 1: I tried to raise the price that we agreed on to increase our profit, but it backfired; they withdrew from the deal and went with our competitor.

Example 2: The plan backfired, instead of gaining clients with our new sales strategy, we actually lost some.

2. v. to bring something/someone to terms

Example 1: In order to bring this deal to terms, we have to agree to their request for free delivery.

Example 2: We started off rocky, but in the end we brought them to terms and agreed to a reasonable contract.

BONUS: **To start off rocky** = to be in disagreement/conflict at first.

3. v. to call the shots / n. a shot caller

Example 1: For all major decisions, please consult with Mr. Lee, he calls the shots around here.

Example 2: We have to wait until the CEO gets back from his business trip before signing, he's the shot-caller.

4. v. to bring something to the table

Example 1: They brought free delivery to the table, so naturally we accepted their offer.

Example 2: Unless you bring a lower price to the table, unfortunately, we will not be doing business with your company.

5. v. to call someone's bluff

Example 1: He said that he would go to our competitor if we didn't lower the price, but we are the only company that offers this service, so we called his bluff and stood firm.

Example 2: They threatened to stop negotiations unless we offered extended warranty, but there was no way that we could do that, so we called their bluff and hoped for the best.

6. v. to cave into someone/something

Example 1: They drove a hard bargain at first, but once the CEO of the company arrived, they caved in to our requests.

Example 2: I wanted pizza for lunch and Mr. Kim wanted a burger, but he caved in to me.

BONUS: **To drive a hard bargain** = to be stubborn about what you want.

7. v. to close a/the deal

Example 1: We closed an important deal last week, so we will have a lot of work ahead of us.

Example 2: The two leaders met to close a deal and sign an accord.

8. v. to come in high/low

Example 1: At first, they came in high, but we were able to bring the price down after some negotiating.

Example 2: We were surprised they came in so low, but we were eager to accept their offer.

9. v. to tiptoe around something/someone

Example 1: The manager is often angry near the end of the month if we have not met our target, so everyone just tiptoes around him.

Example 2: The US government tiptoes around gun laws.

10. n. common ground

Example 1: The client and I share some common ground; we both enjoy playing golf.

Example 2: During the negotiation, we found some common ground; both parties want to have bi-monthly update meetings in Hong Kong.

Part 3

Instructions: Put the following idioms and phrasal verbs in the correct blanks, and in **the correct form**. Some may have more than one possible answer.

1. v. to backfire
2. v. to bring something/someone to terms
3. v. to call the shots / n. a shot caller
4. v. to bring something to the table
5. v. to call someone's bluff
6. v. to cave into someone/something
7. v. to close a/the deal
8. v. to come in high/low
9. n. to tiptoe around something/someone
10. n. common ground

A. We _____ yesterday and we will start work on the new project on the 15th.

B. Even though the two managers are often in disagreement, they do have some _____; they both agree that tardiness cannot be tolerated.

C. Mr. Smith was stubborn at first, but after hours of negotiation, we finally _____.

D. If you want to win this project, you have to _____; it can't just be a one-sided negotiation.

E. We got them _____ and agree to giving us a discounted price.

F. The plan ended up _____, instead of agreeing to the high price we quoted, they ended up backing out completely.

G. The employee said he would quit unless he got a 10% raise, but the manager _____, and in the end, they agreed on a 5% raise.

H. You will need to get the CEO's approval for this, he _____ around here, he's _____.

I. James is not a morning person at all, all of his employees
_____ at least until after lunch time.

J. When negotiating, it's best _____ rather than
low, that way you have the chance to lower your quote and show
that you are willing to compromise.

Part 3 Answers

Instructions: Put the following idioms and phrasal verbs in the correct blanks, and in **the correct form.** Some may have more than one possible answer.

1. v. to backfire
2. v. to bring something/someone to terms
3. v. to call the shots / n. a shot caller
4. v. to bring something to the table
5. v. to call someone's bluff
6. v. to cave into someone/something
7. v. to close a/the deal
8. v. to come in high/low
9. n. to tiptoe around something/someone
10. n. common ground

A. We **closed the deal** yesterday and we will start work on the new project on the 15th.

B. Even though the two managers are often in disagreement, they do have some **common ground**; they both agree that tardiness cannot be tolerated.

C. Mr. Smith was stubborn at first, but after hours of negotiation, we finally **brought him to terms**.

D. If you want to win this project, you have to **bring something to the table**; it can't just be a one-sided negotiation.

E. We got them **to cave in** and agree to give us a discounted price.

F. The plan ended up **backfiring**; instead of agreeing to the high price we quoted, they ended up backing out completely.

G. The employee said he would quit unless he got a 10% raise, but the manager **called his bluff**, and in the end, they agreed on a 5% raise.

H. You will need to get the CEO's approval for this, he **calls the shots** around here, he's **the shot caller**.

I. James is not a morning person at all, and all of his employees **tiptoe around him** at least until after lunch time.

J. When negotiating, it's best **to come in high** rather than low, that way you have the chance to lower your quote, and show that you are willing to compromise.

Part 4

Part 4 - Examples

1. v. to be down to the wire

Example 1: I can't meet you tonight, I'm down to the wire on this project and my boss will kill me if I don't finish it.

Example 2: It's getting down to the wire; if we don't finish this proposal today, we will lose the contract.

2. v. to cover (a lot of) ground

Example 1: Alright, everyone please sit down quickly and open your textbooks, we have a lot of ground to cover today.

Example 2: We covered a lot of ground during our last meeting, we were able to agree and confirm all the payment details.

3. v. to cut someone off

<u>FIRST Meaning</u>: Stop someone from saying something, interrupt.

Example 1: My boss always cuts me off during a presentation, which I don't mind because he knows a lot more about the product than I do.

Example 2: In most cultures, it is extremely rude to cut someone off while they are in the middle of an explanation.

<u>SECOND Meaning</u>: Drive right in front of someone while going fast, giving them little time to brake.

Example 1: The truck cut me off and I ended up swerving to avoid hitting it, which was the cause of the accident.

<u>THIRD Meaning</u>: Stop serving someone drinks.

Example 1: The very drunk man at the bar was cut off, the bartender refused to serve him anymore alcohol.

4. v. to drag on

Example 1: The meeting dragged on since there were so many issues that needed to be cleared up on the agenda.

Example 2: That movie was so boring, it just dragged on, it was two-and-a-half hours long when really they could've done it in just 2 hours.

5. v. to drag one's heels

Example 1: They are dragging their heels on signing the final contract in hopes that they will find a better deal somewhere else.

Example 2: They finally stopped dragging their heels and committed to a 3-year contract.

6. v. to draw the line

Example 1: We can offer a 10% discount, but that's where we draw the line; it would be impossible to go any lower.

Example 2: The manager was very relaxed about people coming to work a little late, but in regards to sexual harassment that's where he drew the line; he had a zero-tolerance policy.

7. v. to drive a hard bargain

Example 1: At first, they drove a hard bargain, but we were able to reason with them and we agreed to mutually beneficial terms.

Example 2: You drive a hard bargain, but given your expertise, we will accept your proposal.

8. v. to drive at something

Example 1: They didn't explicitly say it, but what they were driving at is that our prices compared to our competitor's are extremely high.

Example 2: What are you driving at? Do you mean to say that I am being unfair?

9. v. to fall through

Example 1: The initial proposal fell through; they ended up going with our competitor.

Example 2: My plans for tonight fell through, so would you like to get some dinner together?

10. v. to force someone's hand

Example 1: Initially, I didn't agree with the terms but the manager basically forced my hand and I signed the contract.

Example 2: Even though the employee doesn't want to drink, his supervisor will force his hand.

Part 4

Instructions: Put the following idioms and phrasal verbs in the correct blanks, and in **the correct form**. Some may have more than one possible answer.

1. v. **to be down to the wire**
2. v. **to cover (a lot of) ground**
3. v. **to cut someone off**
4. v. **to drag on**
5. v. **to drag one's heels**
6. v. **to draw the line**
7. v. **to drive a hard bargain**
8. v. **to drive at something**
9. v. **to fall through**
10. v. **to force someone's hand**

A. At first they _____, but in the end they decreased their demands.

B. The CEO basically _____ to give the presentation on my own without him even though I was nervous.

C. We really need to buckle down and focus, we _____ on this project, and if we don't meet the deadline we will lose this customer.

D. The meeting was way longer than it should have been, it just _____ for what seemed like forever.

E. I had _____ my employee as he was about to tell them some confidential information.

F. We tried our best but the deal _____, the customer ended up going with our competitor.

G. Please just give it to me straight, I am trying to understand what _____.

H. The manager is fine with us taking a slightly longer lunch, but arriving late for a meeting, that's where he _____.

I. We just can't get them to sign the contract; we aren't sure why they are _____.

J. Since we have _____ today, I will only be taking questions at the end of my presentation.

Part 4 Answers

Instructions: Put the following idioms and phrasal verbs in the correct blanks, and in **the correct form.** Some may have more than one possible answer.

1. v. to be down to the wire
2. v. to cover (a lot of) ground
3. v. to cut someone off
4. v. to drag on
5. v. to drag one's heels
6. v. to draw the line
7. v. to drive a hard bargain
8. v. to drive at something
9. v. to fall through
10. v. to force someone's hand

A. At first they **drove a hard bargain**, but in the end they decreased their demands.

B. The CEO basically **forced my hand** to give the presentation on my own without him even though I was nervous, and it paid off.

C. We really need to buckle down and focus, we are **down to the wire** on this project, and if we don't meet the deadline we will lose this customer.

D. The meeting was way longer than it should have been, it just **dragged on** for what seemed like forever.

E. I had **to cut off** my employee as he was about to tell them some confidential information.

F. We tried our best but the deal **fell through**, the customer ended up going with our competitor.

G. Please just give it to me straight, I am trying to understand what **you are driving at**.

H. The manager is fine with us taking a slightly longer lunch, but arriving late for a meeting, that's where he **draws the line**.

I. We just can't get them to sign the contract; we aren't sure why they **are dragging their heels**.

J. Since we have **to cover a lot of ground** today, I will only be taking questions at the end of my presentation.

Part 5

Part 5 - Examples

1. n. a gentleman's agreement

Example 1: When we play golf together, we have a gentleman's agreement that the person who wins, uses his winnings to buy dinner and drinks after.

Example 2: We have a gentleman's agreement that whoever arrives late for work must buy coffee for everyone.

2. v. to get behind (a person or idea)

Example 1: Let's see if we can get Company X to get behind the idea of using a 3ʳᵈ party company to handle our customer service.

Example 2: At first, no one agreed with my opinion, but once the manager got behind me, they all *fell in line*.

BONUS: **To fall in line** = to follow what others are doing.

3. v. to get down to business

Example 1: Ok, enough small talk, now it's time to get down to business.

Example 2: We need to get down to business if we intend to meet the project deadline.

4. v. to get the ball rolling

Example 1: Ok, let's brainstorm ideas, James, can you please get the ball rolling?

Example 2: We need to get the ball rolling; we only have this conference hall rented for 1 hour.

5. v. to get the raw end of the deal

Example 1: We got the raw end of the deal, but we really need to keep these clients because they could open up a whole new market for us.

Example 2: We came out extremely successful out of that negotiation; Company A got the raw end of the deal.

6. v. to get through to someone

Example 1: It was difficult at first, but we finally got through to them that our proposal for their machine was the best way to go.

Example 2: I was finally able to get through to John about why being on time is so important; he hasn't been late for work for weeks now.

7. v. to get to the bottom of something

Example 1: We need to get to the bottom of why so many of our machines have been failing.

Example 2: We finally got to the bottom of why Mark seemed so depressed at work these days, It turns out his wife left him.

8. v. to get to the heart of something

Example 1: The heart of the matter is, we can't keep using cheap construction materials; we have to use only high quality.

Example 2: I am not sure why Chad keeps screwing up at work, he's usually a great employee and we need to get to the heart of the matter.

9. v. to give away the farm

Example 1: Jason's negotiation skills are terrible; he basically gives away the farm during each negotiation.

Example 2: We really need to keep this customer, which might mean giving away the farm.

10. v. to give ground

Example 1: The opposing company was playing hardball, but when we offered free delivery, they gave ground.

Example 2: In order for us to give ground on our strict pricing policy, you'll need to place a larger order.

BONUS: **To play hardball** = to be stubborn during a negotiation.

Part 5

Instructions: Put the following idioms and phrasal verbs in the correct blanks, and in **the correct form.** Some may have more than one possible answer.

1. v. a gentleman's agreement
2. v. to get behind (a person or idea)
3. v. to get down to business
4. v. to get the ball rolling
5. v. to get the raw end of the deal
6. v. to get through to someone
7. v. to get to the bottom of something
8. v. to get to the heart of something
9. v. to give away the farm
10. v. to give ground

A. I keep explaining to the engineers exactly what the customer is asking, but they keep misunderstanding, there has to be a way
_____.

B. We really need _____ why our customers are dissatisfied; let's send out a questionnaire in order to get some feedback. (2)

C. At first they were really strict with their demands, but later they _____ and agreed to some of our terms.

D. As long as we can convince the CEO _____ our idea, we can easily have the project funded.

E. Since we really needed this customer to open the door to other companies in the same market, we practically _____ in our negotiation.

F. We finally _____ the machine failure; it hadn't been installed properly. (2)

G. We really _____ in this negotiation, we need to practice our negotiation skills more.

H. Ok, so we have _____, whoever loses this round of golf buys drinks after!

I. Alright, enough small talk, it's time _____.

J. Let's brainstorm some advertising ideas for the GX model before we start the meeting, just _____.

Part 5 Answers

Instructions: Put the following idioms and phrasal verbs in the correct blanks, and in **the correct form.** Some may have more than one possible answer.

1. v. a gentleman's agreement
2. v. to get behind (a person or idea)
3. v. to get down to business
4. v. to get the ball rolling
5. v. to get the raw end of the deal
6. v. to get through to someone
7. v. to get to the bottom of something
8. v. to get to the heart of something
9. v. to give away the farm
10. v. to give ground

A. I keep explaining to the engineers exactly what the customer is asking, but they keep misunderstanding; there has to be a way **to get through to them**.

B. We really need **to get to the bottom of / to get to the heart of** why our customers are dissatisfied; let's send out a questionnaire in order to get some feedback.

C. At first they were really strict with their demands, but later they **gave ground** and agreed to some of our terms.

D. As long as we can convince the CEO **to get behind** our idea, we can easily have the project funded.

E. Since we really needed this customer to open the door to other companies in the same market, we practically **gave away the farm** in our negotiation.

F. We finally **got to the bottom of / to got to the heart of** the machine failure; it hadn't been installed properly.

G. We really **got the raw end of the deal** in this negotiation, we need to practice our negotiation skills more.

H. Ok, so we have **a gentleman's agreement**, whoever loses this round of golf buys drinks after!

I. Alright, enough small talk, it's time **to get down to business**.

J. Let's brainstorm some advertising ideas for the GX model before we start the meeting, just **to get the ball rolling**.

Part 6

Part 6 - Examples

1. v. to go against the grain

Example 1: Since none of the treatments were working, Dr. Johnson decided to go against the grain and try some medicine that wasn't approved yet, and it worked!

Example 2: It goes against the grain to tell outright lies.

2. v. to go back to square one

Example 1: Well, now that this contract fell through, we need to go back to square one and start targeting another company.

Example 2: We can't seem to find the problem with this code, so, it looks like we will need to go back to square one and possibly start over.

3. v. to go back to the drawing board

Example 1: Look guys, this design just isn't working, we need to go back to the drawing board.

Example 2: This approach to the problem isn't working; let's go back to the drawing board.

4. v. to go for broke

Example 1: We went for broke on this last project, but it paid off well and we got a lot of orders lined up.

Example 2: We need to go for broke on this deal; if we get it, it will significantly increase our market share.

5. v. to go over like a lead balloon

Example 1: Our last proposal went over like a lead balloon, the customer hated it.

Example 2: I am not sure if the customer will like our design and proposal, hopefully it doesn't go over like a lead balloon.

6. v. to go over well

Example 1: Our proposal went over well; we will confirm all the contract details during our next conference call.

Example 2: This presentation needs to go over well, a lot of important people will attend the seminar and they could be potential customers.

7. v. to hammer out an agreement

Example 1: Ok, I'm glad we've agreed to work together, now we just need to hammer out all the terms of the agreement.

Example 2: After a few hours of negotiating, we were able to hammer out a deal.

8. adj. hard-nosed

Example 1: The new manager is quite hard-nosed, so don't expect a lot of give and take.

Example 2: During the negotiation, the client was very hard-nosed at first, but he eventually gave ground.

9. v. to have a card up one's sleeve

Example 1: It seems that we are losing the negotiation, but I know that the CEO still has a few cards up his sleeve.

Example 2: We need to have a few cards up our sleeve during this negotiation, just in case they come in playing hardball.

10. v. to hold all the aces/cards/trumps

Example 1: We have no choice but to give in, since they are the only supplier, they hold all the aces.

Example 2: This deal will definitely go through; we hold all the cards, and there is no reason for them to go to the competitor.

Part 6

Instructions: Put the following idioms and phrasal verbs in the correct blanks, and in **the correct form.** Some may have more than one possible answer.

1. v. **to go against the grain**
2. v. **to go back to square one**
3. v. **to go back to the drawing board**
4. v. **to go for broke**
5. v. **to go over like a lead balloon**
6. v. **to go over well**
7. v. **to hammer out an agreement**
8. adj. **to hard-nosed**
9. v. **to have a card up one's sleeve**
10. v. **to hold all the aces/cards/trumps**

A. Andrew decided _____ when he started his new business, it was all or nothing.

B. There's no way I could get an extra vacation day off, my boss is really _____ about that.

C. Since the last design completely failed, we need _____. (2)

D. It _____ to speak out of turn during a meeting in our company, but I had a really good idea and had to voice it.

E. We worked on the sales pitch for this product for months, and we thought it was some of our best work, but in the end, it _____.

F. The two companies decided to work together on this project; all that was left to do was _____.

G. I am sure we will be able to convince this customer to place a large order, I _____ that I am waiting to use just at the right time.

H. Since we _____, this customer will have to agree to or terms since we are the only option for them, no other company provides the service that we do.

I. My presentation _____, the audience thoroughly enjoyed it and I'm sure I impressed a few potential customers at the same time.

Part 6 Answers

Instructions: Put the following idioms and phrasal verbs in the correct blanks, and in **the correct form.** Some may have more than one possible answer.

1. v. to go against the grain
2. v. to go back to square one
3. v. to go back to the drawing board
4. v. to go for broke
5. v. to go over like a lead balloon
6. v. to go over well
7. v. to hammer out an agreement
8. adj. to hard-nosed
9. v. to have a card up one's sleeve
10. v. to hold all the aces/cards/trumps

A. Andrew decided **to go for broke** when he started his new business, it was all or nothing.

B. There's no way I could get an extra vacation day off, my boss is really **hard-nosed** about that.

C. Since the last design completely failed, we need to go back to the drawing board / to go back to square one.

D. It **goes against the grain** to speak out of turn during a meeting in our company, but I had a really good idea and had to voice it.

E. We worked on the sales pitch for this product for months, and we thought it was some of our best work, but in the end, it **went over like a lead balloon**.

F. The two companies decided to work together on this project; all that was left to do was **to hammer out an agreement**.

G. I am sure we will be able to convince this customer to place a large order, I **have a card up my sleeve** that I am waiting to use just at the right time.

H. Since we **hold all the aces**, this customer will have to agree to or terms since we are the only option for them, no other company provides the service that we do.

I. My presentation **went over well**, the audience thoroughly enjoyed it and I'm sure I impressed a few potential customers at the same time.

Part 7

Part 7 - Examples

1. v. to hold out for something/someone

Example 1: We didn't agree to their first proposal because we were holding out for a better offer.

Example 2: I'd like to get married soon, but I am holding out for the perfect guy.

2. v. to hold out on someone

Example 1: Please don't hold out on me. As your manager, I need to know exactly what happened.

Example 2: I'm sorry I held out on you, I should've told you exactly what happened from the beginning.

3. v. to be in the bag

Example 1: This sale is in the bag. Our products are much better and cheaper than those of our competitors.

Example 2: All of our hard work paid off, the contract is in the bag, and we just need to dot the i's and cross the t's.

4. v. to iron something out

Example 1: They have some concerns over the delivery, but I'm sure we can iron them out.

Example 2: Before signing the contract, there were a few issues we had to iron out.

5. v. to knock down the price of something

Example 1: They proposed a pretty high price, but I'm sure we'll be able to knock it down.

Example 2: There has to be a way to knock down the price. If we place a larger order, could you provide a discount?

6. v. to lay one's cards out on the table

Example 1: Ok, I am just going to lay my cards out on the table. The truth is, due to our reduced budget this year, we cannot place an order at this time.

Example 2: I am going to lay my cards out on the table. Due to budgetary cuts, we will not be renewing your contract.

7. v. to make headway

Example 1: We spent all morning on this project and have made headway.

Example 2: In order to make headway on this project, we need to put in a lot more hours into it.

8. v. to nail down the terms of an agreement

Example 1: Ok, it appears we have come to an understanding. Let's nail down the terms of the agreement during the next conference call.

Example 2: We really need to nail down the terms of the agreement soon, before they change their mind and go with a competitor.

9. v. to be off the record

Example 1: The truth is, off the record, the new manager and I don't get along that well.

Example 2: Off the record, if we were to offer you a bigger discount, would you consider being exclusive with us?

10. v. to paint oneself into a corner

Example 1: If they find out that we have been inflating our prices only for them in order to receive a higher margin, then we will have painted ourselves into a corner.

Example 2: We don't want to paint ourselves into a corner, so make sure we do not infringe on any copyright laws or patents.

Part 7

Instructions: Put the following idioms and phrasal verbs in the correct blanks, and in **the correct form.** Some may have more than one possible answer.

1. v. hold out for something/someone
2. v. to hold out on someone
3. v. to be in the bag
4. v. to iron something out
5. v. to knock down the price of something
6. v. to lay one's cards out on the table
7. v. to make headway
8. adj. to nail down the terms of an agreement
9. v. to be off the record
10. v. to paint oneself into a corner

A. I'm not too worried about getting this contract because we are the only providers of this service, so _____.

B. Ok, I'm going _____. Due to budgetary cuts, there's no way we can pay that much. We need a substantial discount if we are to do business together.

C. The contract is almost fully agreed upon, we just have a few kinks _____ .

D. Yes! We were able to get them _____. We went from $1000.00 per unit to $920.00 per unit.

E. This is strictly _____ but just so you know, I don't think that Mr. Smith will be working with us as of next month.

F. We shouldn't agree to their terms so quickly. We need _____ a better offer.

G. In order _____ on this project, we need to delegate some more manpower to it.

H. We don't want to infringe on intellectual property laws, because that would be like _____.

I. We need to get them to quit stalling and finally sit down with us
_____.

J. Are you _____? In order for me to help you properly, you need to tell me the whole truth about what happened.

Part 7 Answers

Instructions: Put the following idioms and phrasal verbs in the correct blanks, and in **the correct form.** Some may have more than one possible answer.

1. v. hold out for something/someone
2. v. to hold out on someone
3. v. to be in the bag
4. v. to iron something out
5. v. to knock down the price of something
6. v. to lay one's cards out on the table
7. v. to make headway
8. adj. to nail down the terms of an agreement
9. v. to be off the record
10. v. to paint oneself into a corner

A. I'm not too worried about getting this contract because we are the only providers of this service, so **it's in the bag**.

B. Ok, I'm going **to lay my cards out on the table**. Due to budgetary cuts, there's no way we can pay that much; we need a substantial discount if we are to do business together.

C. The contract is almost fully agreed upon, we just have a few kinks **to iron out**.

D. Yes! We were able to get them **to knock down the price**. We went from $1000.00 per unit to $920.00 per unit.

E. This is strictly **off the record** but just so you know, I don't think that Mr. Smith will be working with us as of next month.

F. We shouldn't agree to their terms so quickly. We need **to hold out for** a better offer.

G. In order **to make headway** on this project, we need to delegate some more manpower to it.

H. We don't want to infringe on intellectual property laws, because that would be like **painting ourselves into a corner**.

I. We need to get them to quit stalling and finally sit down with us **to nail out the terms of the agreement**.

J. Are you **holding out on me**? In order for me to help you properly, you need to tell me the whole truth about what happened.

Part 8

Part 8 - Examples

1. v. to play hardball

Example 1: Because the last machines that they ordered had some problems, they are playing hardball on this next order.

Example 2: Since they are the only supplier of this equipment, they are able to play hardball.

2. v. to play into someone's hands

Example 1: After our dinner meeting with the clients, they played perfectly into our hands, and we will get this deal for sure now.

Example 2: Our plan worked perfectly. We came in with a very high proposal on purpose, the customers played into our hands, and they negotiated down to our true intended price.

3. v. to pull something off

Example 1: This is the Goliath of our industry, but with our great sales team, we were able to pull off getting them to sign a contract.

Example 2: Even though we were not fully prepared, the presentation went great. I'm glad we were able to pull it off on such short notice.

4. v. to pull something out of a hat

Example 1: We were completely stuck, but suddenly the engineer came up with a great idea. It's like he just pulled it out of a hat.

Example 2: Unless we can pull something out of a hat at the last minute, it looks like this deal will not go through.

5. v. to put one's shoulder to the wheel

Example 1: You can do it! Just put your shoulder to the wheel and I'm sure your presentation will be fine.

Example 2: In order to be successful in life, you need to put your shoulder to the wheel and not give up.

6. v. to raise the ante

Example 1: They raised the ante by offering us their business in China. Now we definitely can't lose this project.

Example 2: Let's raise the ante by letting them know that if they continue to have problems with their machines, we will take our business elsewhere.

7. n. a raw deal

Example 1: We got a raw deal, but we had no choice since they are the only ones currently providing this technology.

Example 2: We're getting a raw deal, but it's only because they have the majority market share and feel that they can treat their customers however they want.

8. v. to reach a stalemate

Example 1: We have reached a stalemate due to some concerns over production cost, but after our next conference call, work should continue.

Example 2: In the contingency that a stalemate is reached due to budgetary issues, the project will be re-evaluated.

9. v. to reach an impasse

Example 1: Since we cannot agree on the terms of the contract, we have reached an impasse, and we have dropped all pursuit of this project.

Example 2: It looks like we have reached an impasse, so unfortunately, we will not be going ahead with this project.

10. v. to read between the lines

Example 1: The director gave a vague response for why the employee was let go, but I was able to read between the lines. He has crossed the line with a female employee.

Example 2: Even though the employee didn't outright say it, I was able to read between the lines and figure out that he will be leaving the company soon.

Part 8

Instructions: Put the following idioms and phrasal verbs in the correct blanks, and in **the correct form**. Some may have more than one possible answer.

1. v. to play hardball
2. v. to play into someone's hands
3. v. to pull something off
4. v. to pull something out of a hat
5. v. to put one's shoulder to the wheel
6. v. to raise the ante
7. n. a raw deal
8. v. to reach a stalemate
9. v. to reach an impasse
10. v. to read between the lines

A. We didn't have a lot of time to prepare, but we were able to _____, and they ended up loving our presentation.

B. They _____. They said that if the machine is not fixed by the end of the month, they will not order from us in the future.

C. The employee got _____ when he negotiated his last contract, but since the unemployment rate was so high, he had no choice but to accept it.

D. I asked my coworker whether he would like to go for lunch with Mr. Smith and me, but he said that he was full. I was able to _____ that he and Mr. Smith don't get along well.

E. Due to high construction costs, we have _____ on this project; we will have to wait until prices go down before continuing.

F. The two managers negotiated for hours, but in regards to being exclusive, they had _____ so they both dropped the possibility of signing a contract.

G. Just _____. if you do so, I am sure you will be able to finish the project before the deadline.

H. The client _____ perfectly, he agreed to make a larger order if we offered a bigger discount. The larger order was what I was hoping for!

I. Mr. Smith is so creative! Whenever there's a problem, he is able to solve it so quickly, and it's like he just _____ solutions _____.

J. Large corporations are able _____ since they have large market share and influence.

Part 8 Answers

Instructions: Put the following idioms and phrasal verbs in the correct blanks, and in **the correct form.** Some may have more than one possible answer.

1. v. to play hardball
2. v. to play into someone's hands
3. v. to pull something off
4. v. to pull something out of a hat
5. v. to put one's shoulder to the wheel
6. v. to raise the ante
7. n. a raw deal
8. v. to reach a stalemate
9. v. to reach an impasse
10. v. to read between the lines

A. We didn't have a lot of time to prepare, but we were able to **pull it off**, and they ended up loving our presentation.

B. They **raised the ante**. They said that if the machine is not fixed by end of the month, they will not order from us in the future.

C. The employee **got a raw deal** when he negotiated his last contract, but since the unemployment rate was so high, he had no choice but to accept it.

D. I asked my coworker whether he would like to go for lunch with Mr. Smith and me, but he said that he was full. I was able to **read between the lines** that he and Mr. Smith don't get along well.

E. Due to high construction costs, we have **reached a stalemate** on this project; we will have to wait until prices go down before continuing.

F. The two managers negotiated for hours, but in regards to being exclusive, they had **reached an impasse**, so they both dropped the possibility of signing a contract.

G. Just **put your shoulder to the wheel**. If you do so, I am sure you will be able to finish the project before the deadline.

H. The client **played into our hands** perfectly, he agreed to make a larger order if we offered a bigger discount. The larger order was what I was hoping for!

I. Mr. Smith is so creative! Whenever there's a problem, he is able to solve it so quickly, and it's like he just **pulls** solutions **out of a hat**.

J. Large corporations are able **to play hardball** since they have large market share and influence.

Part 9

Part 9 - Examples

1. n. a rock-bottom offer

Example 1: After the divorce, the man hit rock bottom and he started drinking every night.

Example 2: I lost all of my money in stocks and I have officially hit rock bottom.

BONUS: **To hit rock bottom** = to be at the lowest point in your life.

2. n. a setback

Example 1: We've had a recent setback when the machine failed, but it should be up and running within the next few days.

Example 2: The high fever returning is a big setback since we thought the antibiotic was working.

3. v. to smooth it over

Example 1: The client was angry about the delivery delay, but we were able to smooth it over by offering a discount on their next order.

Example 2: It looks like we are going to arrive late for dinner, but we can smooth it over by offering to cover the check.

BONUS: **To cover the check** = to pay for a meal.

4. "Speak of the devil"

Example 1: Yes, you're right Michael is a hard worker --- Oh! Speak of the devil, here he comes now!

Example 2: Mr. Smith was looking for you earlier... Oh! Speak of the devil, he's just coming through the door now.

5. v. to stack the deck against someone

Example 1: Tony really had no chance of getting that promotion because he doesn't get along with Mr. Smith. Since he was the deciding factor, the deck was already stacked against him.

Example 2: They tried to stack the deck against me, but I still prevailed and my skills and experience shined through.

6. v. to stand one's ground

Example 1: Even though the other company will try to push a lower discount, just stand your ground and don't give in to their pressure.

Example 2: If you believe you are right, stand your ground and don't let others push you around.

7. v. to stick to one's guns

Example 1: Even though my perspective towards same-sex marriage may be unpopular, I am going to stick to my guns.

Example 2: You may get a lot of criticism during the debate, but don't worry and just stick to your guns.

8. n. a stumbling block

Example 1: We may hit a few stumbling blocks along the way, and that's why we need to arrange a more generous deadline.

Example 2: Well, with the parts delivery being delayed, we have hit a minor stumbling block, but we should still be able to make our deadline.

9. v. to sweeten the deal

Example 1: So, if you were to place a larger order, we would be able to sweeten the deal by giving you a bigger discount.

Example 2: Ok, I can see you are hesitating, so... to sweeten the deal, we will extend our warranty by 6 months.

10. v. to talk someone into/out of something

Example 1: At first, they weren't too keen on releasing that information, but we were able to talk them into it.

Example 2: I know Mr. Smith thinks it's a good idea, but it isn't. Perhaps Larry can talk him out of it since he trusts him.

Part 9

Instructions: Put the following idioms and phrasal verbs in the correct blanks, and in **the correct form.** Some may have more than one possible answer.

1. n. a rock bottom offer
2. n. a setback
3. v. to smooth it over
4. "speak of the devil"
5. v. to stack the deck against someone
6. v. stand one's ground
7. v. to stick to one's guns
8. n. a stumbling block
9. v. to to sweeten the deal
10. v. to talk someone into/out of something

A. Mr. Smith is the CEO of this company. Oh! _____, there he is coming through the entrance.

B. No matter what, don't give in and change your opinion. Just _____. (2)

C. Don't let them bully you into changing your stance. Just _____. (2)

D. They will try _____ by bringing in candidates who already have a relationship with the hiring manager, but just remember, you are more qualified for the position.

E. The parts delivery being late is quite _____ on this project; but we should still be able to make the deadline. (2)

F. Ok, _____, we will throw in free delivery on all orders over $500.00.

G. The machine failure is _____ and we are deeply disappointed, but we guarantee it will be fixed shortly. We apologize for the delay. (2)

H. Henry is planning on changing jobs and moving to Australia. I tried to persuade him not to, but there's just no _____.

I. The client is quite angry once again by the failure of this machine, but if we act quickly and repair it promptly that should _____.

J. I'm about to give you _____, this is sincerely the lowest we can go.

Part 9 Answers

Instructions: Put the following idioms and phrasal verbs in the correct blanks, and in **the correct form.** Some may have more than one possible answer.

1. n. a rock bottom offer
2. n. a setback
3. v. to smooth it over
4. "speak of the devil"
5. v. to stack the deck against someone
6. v. stand one's ground
7. v. to stick to one's guns
8. n. a stumbling block
9. v. to to sweeten the deal
10. v. to talk someone into/out of something

A. Mr. Smith is the CEO of this company. Oh! **Speak of the devil**, there he is coming through the entrance.

B. No matter what, don't give in and change your opinion. Just **stand your ground / stick to your guns**.

C. Don't let them bully you into changing your stance. Just **stand your ground / stick to your guns**.

D. They will try to **stack the deck against you** by bringing in candidates who already have a relationship with the hiring manager, but just remember, you are more qualified for the position.

E. The parts delivery being late is quite **a setback / a stumbling block** on this project, but we should still be able to make the deadline.

F. Ok, **to sweeten the deal**, we will throw in free delivery on all orders over $500.00.

G. The machine failure is **a setback / a stumbling block** and we are deeply disappointed, but we guarantee it will be fixed shortly. We apologize for the delay.

H. Henry is planning on changing jobs and moving to Australia. I tried to persuade him not to, but there's just no **talking him out of it**.

I. The client is quite angry once again by the failure of this machine, but if we act quickly and repair it promptly that should **smooth it over**.

J. I'm about to give you **a rock-bottom offer**, and this is sincerely the lowest we can go.

Part 10

Part 10 - Examples

1. v. to take a stab at something

Example 1: Are you having trouble figuring out how to fix the machine? Here, let me take a stab at it.

Example 2: I think James could be a good manager. There is a position opening up next month, and I am going to tell him to take a stab at it.

2. v. to talk over something

Example 1: Can we set up a meeting for next week? We need to talk over the details of the contract.

Example 2: We need to talk over some of the new policies that will be implemented next week.

3. v. to throw someone a curve

Example 1: My boss really threw me a curve when he called on me to continue his presentation.

Example 2: The weather threw the wedding guests a curve at the outdoor dinner they had planned, and they had to go inside to eat.

4. "to a T"

Example 1: Mr. Smith likes things done to a T. He is super picky.

Example 2: John was able to answer all the interview questions to a T. He is a shoo in for the job.

BONUS: **To be a shoo in** = a candidate is likely to win

5. v. to wax and wane

Example 1: The number of students registered waxes and wanes depending on their schedule.

Example 2: Sales of this product waxes and wanes depending on the economy.

6. v. to wheel and deal

Example 1: Doing business in some developing countries often involves some wheeling and dealing.

Example 2: Wheeling and dealing often involves offering some sort of incentive under the table.

7. "Back to/against the wall"

Example 1: I'm sorry. I tried to save your job but unfortunately, my back is to the wall on this one. You have been late countless times, therefore your last day is on May 1st.

Example 2: The bank has him with his back to the wall. He'll have to pay up now or else he will face bankruptcy.

8. "Beggars can't be choosy"

Example 1: We got a new company jacket recently. It's not really my style, but hey, beggars can't be choosy.

Example 2: The offer they gave us was quite low, but since they were the only ones who contacted us in months, we will have to take it. Beggars can't be choosers!

9. v. to bide your time

Example 1: We need to bide our time before entering a new market, just to make sure the conditions are favorable.

Example 2: The unemployment rate is quite high, so before changing jobs, you should bide your time.

10. n. odds and ends

Example 1: The contract is almost cemented, and we just need to work out the odds and ends.

Example 2: Ok, let's have dinner next week sometime. We can decide the odds and ends on Monday.

BONUS: **To be cemented** = to be established firmly.

Part 10

Instructions: Put the following idioms and phrasal verbs in the correct blanks, and in **the correct form**. Some may have more than one possible answer.

1. v. to take a stab at something
2. v. to talk over something
3. v. to throw someone a curve
4. "to a T"
5. v. to wax and wane
6. v. to wheel and deal
7. "back to/against the wall"
8. "beggars can't be choosy"
9. v. to bide your time
10. n. odds and ends

A. The profit of our corporation _____ depending on the factors that influence our industry.

B. If you put my _____, then I guess I have no choice but to accept your final offer.

C. We can't just jump into a market that we are not properly informed about. We need _____ and wait for the right opportunity.

D. I have a drawer full of _____, so I'm sure you'll be able to find a button in there somewhere.

E. I don't know if I am the right candidate for the job, but I will go to the interview. At least then I can say that I _____.

F. Thomas needs _____ the details of his promotion with his new manager to find out what will be expected of him.

G. The director bought chocolate donuts for everyone, but actually, I don't really like chocolate donuts. I would have preferred vanilla but _____.

H. Unfortunately, we will need _____ during this

negotiation, even though it may not be 100% lawful, it is common practice in this country.

I. During his interview, Mark answered every question _____, so he will definitely get this job.

J. Boy, they really _____! We had no idea they were planning to have the CEO attend the meeting with us. We probably should've been more prepared.

Part 10 Answers

Instructions: Put the following idioms and phrasal verbs in the correct blanks, and in **the correct form.** Some may have more than one possible answer.

1. v. to take a stab at something
2. v. to talk over something
3. v. to throw someone a curve
4. "to a T"
5. v. to wax and wane
6. v. to wheel and deal
7. "back to/against the wall"
8. "beggars can't be choosers"
9. v. to bide your time
10. n. odds and ends

A. The profit of our corporation **waxes and wanes** depending on the factors that influence our industry.

B. If you put my **back against the wall**, then I guess I have no choice but to accept your final offer.

C. We can't just jump into a market that we are not properly informed about. We need **to bide our time and wait** for the right opportunity.

D. I have a drawer full of **odds and ends**, so I'm sure you'll be able to find a button in there somewhere.

E. I don't know if I am the right candidate for the job, but I will go to the interview. At least then I can say that I **took a stab at it**.

F. Thomas needs **to talk over** the details of his promotion with his new manager to find out what will be expected of him.

G. The director bought chocolate donuts for everyone, but actually, I don't really like chocolate donuts. I would have preferred vanilla, but **beggars can't be choosers**.

H. Unfortunately, we will need **to wheel and deal** during this negotiation, and even though it may not be 100% lawful, it is common practice in this country.

I. During his interview, Mark answered every question **to a T**, so he will definitely get this job.

J. Boy, they really **threw us a curve**! We had no idea they were planning to have the CEO attend the meeting with us. We probably should've been more prepared.

Notes

Notes

Notes

Printed in Great Britain
by Amazon